My Phonics
WORD BOOK II

Written by Cass Hollander
Illustrated by Polly Jordan

Published by McClanahan Book Company, Inc. 23 West 26th Street
New York, NY 10010
Printed in the U.S.A.

y

cry
dry
fly
sky
spy
try

cry

Don't **cry**.

sky

Blue as the **sky**

dry

Wash or **dry?**

spy

I **spy**.

fly

Fly away, **fly!**

try

Give it a **try**.

ad

bad
Dad
glad
mad
pad
sad

bad

Too **bad**!

mad

Don't get **mad**.

Dad

Dear old **Dad**!

pad

Grab a **pad**.

glad

Feeling **glad**

sad

So **sad**

aw

draw
law
paw
raw
saw
straw

draw

Color and **draw**.

raw

Eat carrots **raw**.

law

It's the **law**.

saw

Who saw my **saw**?

paw

Shake a **paw**.

straw

Drink with a **straw**.

ay

clay
day
play
say
tray
way

clay

Play with **clay**.

say

What did you **say?**

day

What a great **day**!

tray

Take a **tray**.

play

Come out and **play**!

way

Which **way?**

ed

bed
fed
red
shed
sled
Ted

bed

Time for **bed**.

shed

A garden **shed**

fed

Has the dog been **fed?**

sled

What a fast **sled**!

red

My nose is **red**!

Ted

My bear is named **Ted**.

ip

chip
flip
ship
sip
trip
zip

chip

Eat a **chip**.

sip

Take a **sip**.

flip

Do a **flip**.

trip

Go on a **trip.**

ship

See a **ship**.

zip

Button or **zip**?

it

fit
hit
kit
pit
quit
sit

fit

Does it **fit**?

pit

Peach **pit**

hit

It's a **hit**!

quit

Time to **quit**.

kit

A first-aid **kit**

sit

A place to **sit**

OW

bl**ow**
gr**ow**
l**ow**
r**ow**
sn**ow**
thr**ow**

blow

Blow, wind, **blow**!

row

Ducks in a **row**

grow

Flowers **grow**.

snow

Let it **snow**!

low

Get down **low**.

throw

What a **throw**!

ut

but
cut
nut
rut
shut
strut

GATHER YOUR OWN

but

I like it, **but** . . .

rut

In a **rut**

cut

Scissors **cut**.

shut

Open and **shut**.

nut

Have a **nut**.

strut

Roosters **strut**.

ack

back
crack
pack
quack
snack
track

20

back

Come **back**!

quack

Ducks **quack**.

crack

Step on a **crack**!

snack

Fix a **snack**.

pack

Time to **pack**.

track

Train on the **track**

and

b**and**
gr**and**
h**and**
l**and**
s**and**
st**and**

band

Here comes the **band**!

land

Where can I **land**?

grand

The music is **grand**!

sand

Castles of **sand**

hand

Hand in **hand**

stand

Sit or **stand**?

ave

brave
cave
gave
save
shave
wave

24

brave

Be **brave**.

save

Save, save, save!

cave

What's in this **cave**?

shave

Get a **shave**.

gave

Look what he **gave**.

wave

Smile and **wave**.

ear

clear
dear
ear
hear
near
tear

26

clear

Water is **clear**.

hear

Did you **hear**?

dear

Letters start with **Dear**.

near

Far and **near**

ear

Scratch an **ear**.

tear

Shed a **tear**.

eat

beat
meat
neat
seat
treat
wheat

beat

Beat, beat, beat!

seat

Take a **seat.**

meat

Cut the **meat.**

treat

Trick or **treat?**

neat

Nice and **neat**

wheat

White or **wheat?**

ice

dice
ice
mice
nice
slice
twice

dice

Roll the **dice**.

nice

Very **nice**

ice

Skate on **ice**.

slice

Have a **slice**.

mice

Three blind **mice**

twice

Mice **twice**!

ill

bill
chill
grill
hill
spill
still

bill

Pay the **bill**.

hill

Climb the **hill**.

chill

Feel a **chill**.

spill

Don't **spill**!

grill

Hot off the **grill**

still

Stand **still**.

ine

fine
line
mine
nine
pine
shine

fine

Feeling **fine**

nine

Count to **nine**.

line

Stand in **line**.

pine

Which is **pine**?

mine

Mine, all **mine**!

shine

See them **shine**!

ive

alive
dive
drive
five
hive
jive

alive

It's **alive**!

five

Room for **five**?

dive

Take a **dive**.

hive

Bees in a **hive**

drive

Go for a **drive**.

jive

Jump and **jive**.

old

cold
fold
gold
hold
old
told

cold

Brrrr . . . It's **cold**!

hold

A hand to **hold**

fold

Wash and **fold**.

old

How **old**?

gold

A crown of **gold**

told

Our story is **told**.

one

al**one**
b**one**
c**one**
ph**one**
st**one**
t**one**

alone

All **alone**

phone

Answer the **phone**.

bone

Give a dog a **bone**.

stone

Step on a **stone**.

cone

Ice cream **cone**

tone

A nice **tone**

orn

born
corn
horn
thorn
torn
worn

42

born

When were you **born?**

thorn

Ouch! A **thorn!**

corn

Mmmm . . . fresh **corn!**

torn

This page is **torn.**

horn

Blow your **horn!**

worn

My shoes are **worn.**

ump

bump
dump
jump
plump
pump
stump

bump

What a bad **bump**!

plump

Nice and **plump**

dump

Visit the **dump**.

pump

Work the **pump**.

jump

Jump . . . jump . . . jump!

stump

Jump over the **stump**!

unk

bunk
chunk
dunk
junk
skunk
trunk

bunk

Take the top **bunk**.

junk

What *is* all this **junk**?

chunk

Have a **chunk**.

skunk

Oh, no! A **skunk**!

dunk

Cookies to **dunk**

trunk

An elephant's **trunk**

eel

feel
heel
kneel
peel
steel
wheel

feel

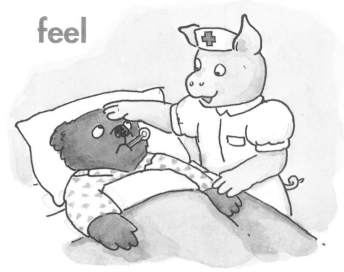

How do you **feel**?

peel

A banana **peel**

heel

Such a high **heel**!

steel

Strong as **steel**

kneel

Always **kneel**.

wheel

Turn the **wheel**!

ike

alike
bike
hike
like
spike
strike

50

alike

Dressed **alike**

like

What I **like**!

bike

Ride a **bike**.

spike

Hit a **spike**.

hike

Take a **hike**.

strike

It's a **strike**!

oat

boat
coat
float
goat
moat
throat

boat

Row the **boat**.

goat

Feed a **goat**.

coat

Button your **coat**.

moat

Fill the **moat**.

float

Will it **float**?

throat

Sore **throat**

oil

boil
broil
foil
oil
soil
spoil

boil

When will it **boil**?

oil

The car needs **oil**.

broil

Burgers to **broil**

soil

Dig in the **soil**.

foil

Wrap it in **foil**.

spoil

Milk can **spoil**.

ole

hole
mole
pole
role
sole
stole

hole

Dig a **hole**.

role

Playing a **role**

mole

It's a **mole**!

sole

A flapping **sole**

pole

Flag on a **pole**

stole

Guess what they **stole**?

ool

cool
fool
pool
school
stool
tool

cool

Too **cool**!

school

Go to **school**.

fool

Act like a **fool**.

stool

Sit on a **stool**.

pool

Jump in the **pool**!

tool

Use a **tool**.

ose

close
hose
nose
pose
rose
those

close

Open or **close**?

pose

Strike a **pose**.

hose

Garden **hose**

rose

Smell a **rose**.

nose

Funny **nose**

those

These or **those**?

ound

f**ound**
gr**ound**
h**ound**
p**ound**
r**ound**
s**ound**

unch

b**unch**
cr**unch**
h**unch**
l**unch**
m**unch**
p**unch**

found

Look what I **found**!

pound

Pound, **pound**, **pound**!

ground

Sit on the **ground**.

round

Bubbles are **round**.

hound

Stop that **hound**!

sound

Don't make a **sound**!

bunch

A silly **bunch**!

lunch

Stop for **lunch**.

crunch

Carrots **crunch**.

munch

Good to **munch**

hunch

Have a **hunch**.

punch

Make some **punch**.

Phonogram stickers
Help your child press out the stickers and place them on the correct pages.

ip

ave

y

it

ear

ad

ow

eat

aw

ut

ice

ay

ack

ill

ed

and

ine

ive	unk	ole
old	eel	ool
one	ike	ose
orn	oat	ound
ump	oil	unch

ose

ound

unch